*To My Special
friend Elizabeth*

Hygge

COMFORT & FOOD FOR THE SOUL

*♡ with
love and a
lot of (Hygge)
♡*

 **CookNation**

Hygge: Comfort & Food For The Soul

A cosy collection of comfort food, drinks & lifestyle recipes for you, your friends & family to enjoy.

Credits: imagery under license from Shutterstock

ISBN 978-1-911219-55-2

• •

CookNation

BELL & MACKENZIE
PUBLISHING LIMITED

www.bellmackenzie.com

Contents

Hygge recipes: bakes, sweets & jam

Hygge recipes: drinks

Hygge recipes: cakes & puddings

Hygge craft

Hygge yoga

The moments of happiness we enjoy take us by surprise. It is not that we seize them, but that they seize us.

Ashley Montagu

Introduction

"Hygge is only ever meant to be felt, not explained"

It is often said hygge (pronounced 'hoo-ga') is lost in translation, that there is no one word in the English dictionary with which to adequately define it. Whilst definition is to some extent necessary, the Danes like to think that hygge is only ever meant to be felt, not explained.

It is this feeling which is so deeply engrained in the Danish psyche and way of life that contributes to making Denmark officially one of the happiest places on earth. The pursuit of hygge is a way of life for the Danes.

What Is Hygge?

There are many words and terms which can be used to describe hygge – cosiness, comfort, contentment, bliss, happiness, warmth, friendship, family, gratitude, appreciation of simplicity and the here & now. Hygge can be tasted, seen, heard and felt – it affects all our senses. Hygge is being snug, secure and safe. All are accurate yet none individually encompass what can only be expressed in a single word - 'hygge'.

Hygge can be many things to many people and to that end it is personal but also ultimately sociable so you can share the feeling and mood with friends. It is a genuine pleasure in appreciating a moment - experiencing and feeling it. It is an ambience, a mood, an attitude - even a formula for life.

Hygge is warm drinks, comfortable clothes, beautifully lit rooms, candles, blankets, conversation, walks through the forest as autumn leaves fall, dinner, warmth by a fire as a storm rages outside...the list goes on.

It is contentment and appreciation.

Why Do We Need Hygge?

Life needs moments of pleasure - the more the better. Pleasure brings happiness and ultimately contentment. To seek out and embrace these moments of pleasure brings focus to our lives which is not centered around the material gain. The mindfulness nature of hygge is both grounding and humbling – it is the ultimate feel-good factor.

By pursuing hygge as a way of life, moments of stress, worry and concern can be replaced. Phones, laptops and social media are not part of hygge, these things only serve distract from the ultimate goal of being in the moment and enjoying it fully.

Comfort Food

Comfort food, especially in the darker months of the year is quintessentially hygge. Food that warms the soul, evokes moods of happiness and contentment, awakens the taste buds to pleasure and memories of childhood.

It's not just the food itself that is hygge, but how it is eaten, whether with friends and family in conversation around the table or tucked up under a blanket on a bleak winter's afternoon sipping warm fruit punch in front of the fire. That warm and fuzzy feeling that is hygge is created with unpretentious yet delicious fare that fits the moment.

Hygge food should be a treat, not concerned with the limits of healthy nutrition but a welcome break from the norm – not extravagant but immensely gratifying.

Try our selection of some of the best comfort foods for instant hygge happiness from heart warming soups and stews to sweet bakes & puddings, home baked breads and jams to seasonal mulled wines and decadent hot chocolate.

Food that is hygge is a welcome diversion from healthy eating. It's time to let your guard down and treat yourself and the company you are in. Fussy & fancy food is not hygge but that does not mean Hygge food is plain. It should be delicious, hearty, warming comforting and sometimes naughty. Hygge food should be made with love.

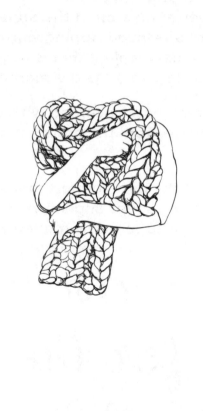

Indulgent Hygge

"Don't underestimate the value of doing nothing, of just going along, listening to all the things you can't hear, and not bothering."

Winnie The Pooh

Indulgent Hygge

Hygge is not always planned or created it just happens, it's a mood that you feel often without warning - that's what makes it so nice. That said there are situations where indulgent hygge moments are required to soothe you and help you unwind, forget about what needs to be done and focus on the moment.

To that end, here are some all-year-round simple pleasures to fall back on that will give instant and maximum pleasure.

Eat Cake

Cake is hygge. Eat it when you want. It's comforting like nothing else. Be generous – if you want a large piece, have it. Savour it, and the moment with no guilt - just the pure pleasure of eating cake.

If you want a second piece - that's ok too!!

Rainy Day Sanctuary

Pulling some cosy blankets over your head as you hear the rain against the window makes you appreciate your cosiness even more. The sound is soothing and your bed feels like a sanctuary. Is there any place you would rather be?

Take A Candlelit Bath

A soak in the tub is one of life's pleasures and very hygge. It's indulgent for one but can also be cosy for two!

Make sure there is plenty of hot water and that anybody you share your home with is not going to disturb you.

Turn off your mobile and take the phone off the hook.

Run your bath at hot as you wish adding cold towards the end to get the temperature just right. Add your favourite bubbles or essential oils like lavender or chamomile.

Have the softest towel and your bathrobe draped over the radiator so they are warm and cosy.

Light some candles.

Step in, slip into the glorious warmth and relax. Try to clear your mind and take in the moment.

When you think it's time to get out....don't. Top up with a little more hot water and indulge yourself for a little longer.

When you've finished your luxurious soak, slip on your bathrobe, put the kettle on and find your special hygge corner and savour the moment with a your favourite magazine or book.

Music

The joy of putting a classic album on, sitting back in a cosy armchair and just listening is something we rarely do. Often music is just background noise. Rediscover 'really' listening one afternoon in a hygge nook of your house.

The whole word is a series of miracles - but we're so used to them we call them ordinary things.

Hans Christian Anderson

Feel-Good Film Time

So much of our lives involve organising, arranging and fitting in around others. Sometimes it's lovely to be able to do something for yourself at a time when you wouldn't normally dream of it. Watching a movie is always nice but it doesn't always have to be at the weekend or in the evening.

Put the laundry, dishes, cleaning and any other daily chores on hold for a couple of hours and choose a feel-good film to watch in the morning. Get a blanket or bring down your duvet and have some of your favourite popcorn within arms reach. It's naughty and indulgent and normally completely against the rules – especially on a weekday. Part of hygge is being a little sinful now again. Watch alone or with friends and family who'll love you for it.

Take In The View

Choose the best window in your house. Pull up a chair and take in the view with a cosy jumper, thick socks and a hot chocolate. Of course not everyone will have a gorgeous view of the countryside but there is beauty all around. Open your eyes to the tiny details of life.

"Joy comes to us in ordinary moments. We risk missing out when we get too busy chasing down the extraordinary."

Brene Brown

Outdoor Hygge

"A woodland in full colour is awesome as a forest fire, in magnitude at least, but a single tree is like a dancing tongue of flame to warm the heart."

Hal Borland

Outdoor Hygge

While the home may be your comfort central, hygge is not limited to the indoors. Venturing outdoors and making a special connection with nature and the present moment is precious. Moreover the experience of connecting outdoors makes returning home to a hygge haven even nicer.

Hygge outdoors can take many forms. It may be an autumnal walk through the leaves with hat, gloves and scarf or creating a beautiful fairylight snug in the corner of your garden with a blanket nearby and a cup of cocoa to sit and watch the world go by with.

Outdoor hygge is not just limited to the colder months: hygge in summer can be just as rewarding with outdoor barbeques, candles and soft music whether it be in your own garden or a weekend away with family and friends.

If you are lucky enough to have a garden or outdoor space it can be the perfect setting to indulge in nature. Sights, smells and sounds all contribute to perfect hygge and so does the warmth of light.

Try some of the ideas on the following pages to make the most of the outdoors and reconnecting with nature.

Lighting

Lighting and ambience is key to hygge. Indoor mood lighting can be easier to achieve thanks to varying watts of light bulbs, dimmer switches, lamp shades and the like but outdoor lighting can be just as effective.

Lanterns & Table Top Lamps

These come in many shapes and sizes from the traditional storm type lanterns and mosaic covered lamps to more modern soft light globes. Try experimenting using a mix of old and new. Most will take a simple traditional tea light, battery operated tea light or may even be solar powered. Never place candles underneath a shelf or too close to a plant or any object that could catch light. Remember to extinguish all candles safely even if they are being left outside.

Candles

Candles as we know are big on the hygge list. There are a number of great quality garden candles that range from small to giant with thick wicks that can withstand blustery winds. Try dotting these around a patio close to potted scented herbs or shrubs like lavender and rosemary or to highlight a beautifully scented climber like honeysuckle.

"Thousands of candles can be lit from a single candle, and the life of the candle will not be shortened. Happiness never decreases by being shared."
Buddha

Fairylights

So magical no matter your age. These can be draped on walls, fences, hung from trees or laid on the ground and are the perfect ambiance setter. Use lights that are suitable for outdoor use (not the ones from your Christmas tree), opt for soft glow rather than harsher LED lights and experiment with different colours.

Soft Furnishings

Hygge outdoors should be comfortable but that doesn't mean it can be limited only to the warmer months of the year. Socialising with friends and family outdoors can be done and enjoyed even in winter. Bring out your summer garden table and chairs with some furniture throws, inside cushions and blankets and you will soon have a welcoming and cosy area. There is something so lovely about feeling the cold on your cheeks while underneath a blanket in the warm glow of a candle.

Firepit/Chiminea

For many of us the beauty of an indoor fire or wood-burning stove is not practical but if you are lucky to have outdoor space then creating the warmth of a fire outdoors is the next best thing. Of course building your own from stray rocks around the garden can work but we recommend the simplicity of a firepit or chininea. They are sturdy and effective and provide a beautiful focal point to a garden gathering no matter what time of year. Add marshmallows and hot chocolate to complete the hygge moment. Be careful of children when having outdoor fires.

"The fire is the main comfort of the camp, whether in summer or winter, and is about as ample at one season as at another. It is as well for cheerfulness as for warmth and dryness."

Henry David Thoreau

Walking

There are few better activities to appreciate a beautiful day than a walk. Any season will bring rewards: the exciting prospect of life on a spring morning, the feeling of opportunity as the sun begins to radiate heat on a summer's day, the unmistakable smell of falling leaves in a woodland setting in autumn or the feeling that it might just snow as you take a brisk walk on a winter's afternoon before the sun sets.

Walking really does make you appreciate the moment in true hygge style. There are so many treats for your eyes as well as the smells and sound of the seasons. Walks such as these can be appreciated alone or with company and with a cosy hygge set-up waiting for you back home, the day couldn't be better.

Driftwood

Collecting driftwood is one of life's pleasures. The shapes, colours and textures of seasoned wood are art forms. Children and adults alike can appreciate combing a beach to find the most interesting treasures in this year-round activity. You don't need to live by the coast to participate; lakes, lochs and rivers will all uncover wonderful gems which you can either take home for indoor and outdoor decoration or to dry off as kindling for the fire – perfect!

"I promise myself that I will enjoy every minute of the day that is given me to live."

Thich Nhat Hanh

Outdoor Clothing

To be hygge-happy you need to feel comfortable, at ease, cosy in your clothing and always casual – smart dressing takes a little too much effort and is not so hygge. For the colder months think oversized woollen jumpers, warm socks, scarves (the longer and thicker the better), woolly hats, beanies and of course gloves. Find a great pair of gloves that really fit - not the pair you hurriedly bought in a discount store on the worst day of winter last year. Wear worn-in, comfy footwear like trainers where the weather permits and always layers - being cold is definitely not hygge.

In warmer months, again keep it casual and loose but be prepared for changes so summer cardigans will always be a hygge winner.

Bike Rides

In Denmark, the home of hygge, bikes are commonplace both as a mode of transport to and from work and just for fun. In countries where bicycle culture is not so engrained in society we can often forget the joy of two wheels. Being so close to the elements and feeling the wind through you hair is a lovely way to feel uninhibited. Wrap up in the winter and strip down in the summer, the sense of freedom on a bike is very hygge. It's social and perfect for a fun afternoon with friends and family. Breathe it in with every twist, turn, climb and descent. Finish off with coffee, cake and chat.

Early Morning

Recipes

Maple Syrup Pancake Stack

SERVES TWO

INGREDIENTS

- 175g/6oz plain flour
- 2 eggs
- 50g/2oz melted butter
- 250ml/1 cup milk
- 50g/2oz sugar
- 1 tsp vanilla extract
- ½ tsp salt
- 3 tsp baking powder
- Olive oil
- Maple syrup to serve
- Fresh berries to serve
- Greek yoghurt to serve

HYGGE HINT

If friends are staying over just double the quantities. The smell of homemade pancakes will entice everyone into the kitchen. Turn on the oven and keep the pancakes warm while you make another batch!

THE METHOD

1 Beat the eggs and sugar together in a bowl. Add the melted butter and keep beating for a minute or two. Add the vanilla extract & milk and carry on beating. Sift the flour into the bowl. Add the salt and whisk together until everything is nice and smooth.

2 Add a couple of drops of olive oil to the frying pan. Let the pan heat up and then use a ladle to scoop out some of the pancake batter (about 2 tbsp per pancake).

3 Pour it into the pan, cook for a minute or two and then flip over. Cook until both sides are golden brown.

4 Serve with maple syrup, yoghurt & fresh berries.

Cinnamon Porridge

SERVES ONE

INGREDIENTS

- 50g/2oz porridge oats
- ½ tsp cinnamon
- 2 tsp brown sugar
- 250ml/1 cup milk
- 2 tbsp Greek yogurt
- 1 tbsp honey

THE METHOD

1 Combine together the oats, cinnamon, sugar & milk over a gentle heat and cook for 3-4 mins.

2 When the porridge is ready pour into a bowl and dollop the yoghurt on top. Drizzle the honey over and serve.

HYGGE HINT

Porridge is traditionally comforting - thick, stodgy, sweet and filling. Cupping a warm bowl of porridge in your hands in the morning as you ponder the day ahead is hygge at its best.

Raspberry Overnight Oats

SERVES TWO

INGREDIENTS

- 100g/3½oz oats
- 75g/3oz raspberries
- 1 pear, peeled, cored & chopped
- 180ml/¾ cup milk
- 1 tbsp Greek yoghurt
- 1 tbsp honey

THE METHOD

1 Spread the oats out in the base of an airtight lunch box.

2 Place all the other ingredients into a blender or food processor and blend until smooth.

3 Pour the blended raspberries on top of the oats. Close the lunch box over and store in the fridge overnight. Enjoy in the morning.

HYGGE HINT

This is a great way to start your day. It's fresh and filling and sets you up for the morning ahead.

Sweet Potato Hash

SERVES TWO

INGREDIENTS

- 2 tbsp olive oil
- 4 sausages
- 1 onion, sliced
- 1 red pepper, de-seeded & sliced
- 1 large sweet potato
- 2 free-range eggs

HYGGE HINT

A simple, hearty hygge start to the day.

THE METHOD

1 Peel and finely grate the sweet potato. Using some kitchen roll pat off any excess moisture.

2 Meanwhile heat the oil in a frying pan, add sausages and cook for a few minutes until they are browned.

3 Add the onions, peppers and sweet potato and sauté for 8-12 minutes or until everything is cooked through. Crack the eggs into the pan, cover and leave to gently continue cooking whilst the eggs set.

4 Season well and serve.

Stews, Soups & Meals

Recipes

Pork & Cloudy Cider Casserole

SERVES FOUR

INGREDIENTS

- 900g/2lb pork tenderloin, cubed
- 4 garlic cloves, crushed
- 200g/7oz dried apricots, finely chopped
- 250ml/1 cup dry cloudy cider
- 250ml/1 cup chicken stock
- 3 tbsp plain/all purpose flour
- 2 onions, chopped
- 2 parsnips, very finely chopped
- 2 celery stalks, chopped
- 800g/1lb tinned flageolet beans, drained
- 2 tbsp freshly chopped flat leaf parsley
- Olive oil
- Salt & pepper to taste

THE METHOD

1 Preheat the oven to 180C/350F/Gas Mark 4.

2 Place the cubed pork in a plastic bag with the flour and shake well to cover the meat. Quickly brown the pork in a frying pan in some olive oil for a few minutes.

3 Add all the ingredients, except the chopped parsley, to an oven-proof dish. Season well, cover, place in the oven and cook for 1-1½ hours or until the meat & vegetables are tender.

4 Ensure the dish doesn't dry up by adding a little more stock during cooking if needed. Sprinkle with chopped parsley and serve.

HYGGE HINT

Pork and cider are best friends. The sweetness of the apricots in this dish gives it that hygge edge. Increase quantities proportionally if entertaining larger numbers. Wash down with locally brewed cider or organic apple juice.

Chocolate & Cinnamon Chilli

SERVES FOUR

INGREDIENTS

- Olive oil
- 900g/2lb lean, minced/ground beef
- 1 cinnamon stick
- 1 tsp each ground cumin & chilli powder
- 1½ tbsp cocoa powder
- 350g/12oz carrots, cut into batons
- 2 onions, chopped
- 400g/14oz ripe tomatoes, chopped
- 4 garlic cloves, crushed
- 1 tbsp dried basil
- 2 tbsp tomato puree/paste
- 250ml/1 cup beef stock
- 350g/12oz rice
- Salt & pepper to taste

HYGGE HINT

Sometimes making food hygge means adding something extra and making the dish a little decadent & indulgent while not being overly fancy.

THE METHOD

1 Preheat the oven to 200C/400F/Gas Mark 6.

2 Gently sauté the onion, garlic, spices & herbs in some olive oil for a few minutes until softened.

3 Add all the other ingredients, except the cinnamon stick, and cook for 4-5 minutes longer.

4 Combine well in an oven-proof dish, add the cinnamon stick, cover and cook in the oven for 30-40 minutes or until the mince is cooked through and the stock is absorbed.

5 Meanwhile cook the rice in salted boiling water until tender.

6 Remove the cinnamon stick and serve the chilli piled on top of the drained rice.

Beef & Shallot Casserole

INGREDIENTS

- 1.5kg/3lb 6oz beef stewing steak
- 450g/1lb shallots, chopped
- 2 garlic cloves, crushed
- 1 red onion, chopped
- 350g/12oz baby carrots, halved lengthways
- 350g/12oz parsnips, halved lengthways
- 2 celery sticks, chopped
- 200g/7oz chestnut mushrooms, sliced
- 500ml/2 cups beef stock/broth
- 1 tbsp each freshly chopped thyme & flat leaf parsley
- Olive oil
- Salt & pepper to taste

HYGGE HINT

When you've prepped this dish and popped it into the oven, take the family for a good long walk and enjoy the outdoors.

THE METHOD

1 Preheat the oven to 140C/275F/ Gas Mark 1. First cube the beef and quickly brown in a frying pan with a little olive oil on a high heat for a minute or two. You'll need to do this in batches.

2 Remove from the heat, set the beef aside and use the same pan to gently sauté the red onions, mushrooms, garlic, celery, shallots, carrots & parsnips for a few minutes in a little more oil.

3 Add all the ingredients, except the chopped parsley, to an oven-proof dish. Cover tightly and leave to cook for 3-3½ hours or until the beef is tender and cooked through.

4 At the end of this time remove a large handful of vegetables along with as much of the stock as possible and blend these together in a blender to make a thick 'gravy' – add more stock if you need to 'loosen' it up a little.

5 Stir this gravy back into the casserole and serve.

Sun-dried Tomato Cottage Pie

SERVES FOUR

INGREDIENTS

- 900g/2lb lean, ground/minced beef
- 2 onions, chopped
- 300g/11oz carrots, chopped
- 200g/7oz mushrooms, sliced
- 2 celery sticks, chopped
- 2 tbsp sun-dried tomato puree/ paste
- 4 sun-dried tomatoes from a jar, finely chopped
- 200g/7oz tinned chopped tomatoes
- 2 garlic cloves, crushed
- 2 tsp dried mixed herbs
- 60ml/¼ cup beef stock/broth
- 1.35kg/3lb desiree potatoes, peeled & cubed
- Splash of milk
- Large knob of butter
- Olive oil
- Salt & pepper to taste

HYGGE HINT

This dish gets a Mediterranean twist. The sun-dried tomatoes are sweet to the taste buds which compliment the beef.

THE METHOD

1 Preheat the oven to 200C/400F/Gas Mark 6. Quickly brown the mince in a frying pan with some olive oil on a high heat for a minute or two.

2 Reduce the heat, add the onions, carrots, mushrooms, celery & garlic and gently sauté for a few minutes along with the mince.

3 Stir in the sun-dried tomatoes and paste, chopped tomatoes, stock and mixed herbs. Season, simmer for 10 minutes and then combine all the ingredients, except the potatoes, milk & butter, into an oven-proof dish.

4 Meanwhile make the mash by cooking the potatoes in salted boiling water until tender.

5 Drain the potatoes, add a splash of milk along with the butter and mash until smooth.

6 Spread the mash over cover the cooked mince in the oven-proof dish.

7 Place in the oven and leave to cook for 30-40 minutes, or until the beef is tender and cooked through.

Nutmeg Double Cheese Mac

SERVES FOUR

INGREDIENTS

- 500g/1lb 2oz macaroni pasta
- 2 tbsp dijon mustard
- 250ml/1 cup crème fraiche
- 6 tbsp milk
- ½ tsp nutmeg
- 200g/7oz grated mature cheddar cheese
- 200g/7oz grated double Gloucester cheese
- 125g/4oz spinach, chopped
- Salt & pepper to taste

THE METHOD

1 Preheat the oven to 200C/400F/Gas Mark 6.

2 Cook the pasta in salted boiling water until tender.

3 Meanwhile gently warm through the mustard, crème fraiche, milk, nutmeg and cheeses in a saucepan.

4 Combine all the ingredients in an oven-proof dish. Season well, cover and place in the oven for 30-40 minutes or until piping hot.

HYGGE HINT

Double cheese is always comforting - especially in mac cheese. The nutmeg gives it an extra seasonal twist too. This is real comfort food, made with love. For a hygge night in, have everyone on the sofa with a movie ready to play, fire on, dim the lights and serve up in warm bowls.

Red Wine & Beef Casserole

SERVES FOUR

INGREDIENTS

- 1.5kg/3lb 6oz beef stewing steak
- 2 onions, chopped
- 2 tbsp plain/all purpose flour
- 250ml/1 cup beef stock/broth
- 250ml/1 cup red wine
- 300g/11oz carrots, chopped
- 150g/5oz spinach leaves
- 3 tbsp horseradish sauce
- 200g/7oz chestnut mushrooms
- 1 tbsp freshly chopped oregano
- Olive oil
- Salt & pepper to taste

HYGGE HINT

Hearty meals like this seem to taste so much better when you've had a day outdoors. While it's cooking take out your bicycle and go for a bracing ride.

THE METHOD

1 Preheat the oven to 140C/275F/Gas Mark 1.

2 Quickly brown in a high-sided frying pan with a little olive oil, on a high heat for a minute or two.

3 Reduce the heat, add the onions, carrots & mushrooms and sauté for a few minutes with the beef. Add more oil if needed.

4 Stir in the flour and cook for a minute or two longer.

5 Stir in the red wine & stock and combine all the ingredients into an oven-proof dish. Season, cover tightly and leave to cook for 2-2½ hours or until the beef is tender and cooked through.

Stovies

SERVES FOUR

INGREDIENTS

- 750g/1lb 11oz skinless chicken breasts
- 900g/2lb desiree potatoes, peeled & cubed
- 200g/7oz pancetta cubes
- 2 onions
- 2 tbsp Worcestershire sauce
- 320ml/1½ cups chicken stock
- Olive oil
- Salt & pepper to taste

HYGGE HINT

Stovies is a classic Scottish dish, traditionally made using left over roast beef or lamb. The Scots know a thing or two about hygge.

THE METHOD

1 Preheat the oven to 200C/400F/Gas Mark 6

2 First cook the chicken breasts under a medium grill for 15-25 minutes or until cooked through.

3 Shred the meat with two forks and set to one side.

4 Meanwhile sauté the pancetta and onions in a frying pan with some olive oil for a few minutes.

5 Add all the ingredients to an oven-proof dish and combine. Season well, cover and cook in the oven for 40-60 minutes or until the potatoes are tender.

6 Ensure the dish doesn't dry up by adding a little more stock during cooking if needed. Serve with lots of black pepper.

Comforting Toad In The Hole

SERVES FOUR

INGREDIENTS

- 10 thick, pork sausages
- 250g/9oz plain/all-purpose flour
- 4 free range eggs
- 500ml/2 cups milk
- 1 tbsp dijon mustard
- 1 tsp each of dried thyme and rosemary
- 2 large onions thinly sliced into half moons
- 2 x 400g/14oz tins baked beans
- Olive oil
- Salt & pepper to taste

HYGGE HINT

Toad In The Hole - hearty simple comfort food.

THE METHOD

1 Preheat the oven to 180C/350F/Gas Mark 4.

2 Pierce the sausages and put in an oven-proof dish with a oil.

3 Cook for 8-12 minutes or until the sausages are browned. Add the onions for the last 6 minutes of cooking so that they begin to tenderise.

4 Meanwhile make up the batter by sifting the flour into a bowl. Beat the eggs into the flour and gradually add the milk, beating all the time to create a smooth batter. Add the dried herbs, mustard and seasoning.

5 Split the cooked sausages lengthways and arrange, along with the onions in the oven-proof dish. Pour the batter over the top and cook for a further 25-35 minutes or until the batter is golden brown and puffed up.

6 Heat the baked beans in a saucepan and serve with the toad in the hole.

Warming Pumpkin Seed Soup

SERVES FOUR

INGREDIENTS

- 1 tbsp olive oil
- 1 tbsp dried pumpkin seeds, chopped
- 650g/1lb 7oz pumpkin flesh, peeled and cubed
- 200g/7oz potatoes, peeled and cubed
- 1lt/4 cups vegetable stock/broth
- 120ml/½ cup single cream
- Salt & pepper to taste

THE METHOD

1 Add all the ingredients to a saucepan, except the pumpkin seeds and cream.

2 Cover and leave to gently simmer for 20 minutes or until everything is tender and cooked through.

3 Use a blender to blend until smooth.

4 Return to the pan, stir through the cream and gently warm for a minute or two.

5 Adjust the seasoning and serve with the pumpkin seeds sprinkled on top.

HYGGE HINT

At Halloween buy an extra pumpkin - one to carve on Halloween night and the other to make this delicious soup. Pour into a flask and take with you trick or treating.

Sweet Carrot & Honey Soup

SERVES FOUR

INGREDIENTS

- 1 tbsp olive oil
- 2 leeks, sliced
- 650g/1lb 7oz carrots, chopped
- 1 tbsp honey
- 1 bay leaf (remove before blending)
- ½ tsp crushed chilli flakes
- 1lt/4 cups vegetable stock/broth
- 120ml/½ cup single cream
- Salt & pepper to taste

HYGGE HINT

*Serve on a rainy day in mugs
huddled on the sofa.*

THE METHOD

1 Gently sauté the chopped leeks in the olive oil for a few minutes until softened.

2 Add all the ingredients to a saucepan. except the cream. Cover and leave to gently simmer for 20 minutes or until everything is tender and cooked through.

3 Remove the bay leaf and use a blender to blend until smooth.

4 Return to the pan, stir through the cream and gently warm for a minute or two. Adjust the seasoning and serve.

Winter Cauli & Stilton Soup

SERVES FOUR

INGREDIENTS

- 1 tbsp olive oil
- 1 onion, chopped
- 1lt/4 cups vegetable stock/broth
- 2 celery sticks, chopped
- 1 leek, chopped
- 200g/7oz potatoes, peeled & cubed
- 1 bay leaf (remove before blending)
- 600g/1lb 5oz cauliflower florets
- 120ml/½ cup single cream
- 125g/4oz stilton cheese
- 2 tbsp freshly chopped chives
- Salt & pepper to taste

THE METHOD

1 Gently sauté the chopped leeks and onions in the olive oil for a few minutes until softened.

2 Add all the ingredients, except the cream and chives, to a saucepan. Cover and leave to gently simmer for 20-30 minutes or until everything is tender and cooked through.

3 Remove the bay leaf and use a blender to blend until smooth.

4 Stir through the cream and leave to warm for minute or two.

5 Adjust the seasoning and serve with the chopped chives sprinkled over the top.

HYGGE HINT

This is a wonderful thick and satisfying soup. For a casual get-together with friends, serve with chunky crusty bread torn from a good quality loaf. Light a few candles on the kitchen table too - it'll warm your soul.

Cannellini & Sausage Bake

SERVES FOUR

INGREDIENTS

- 12 thick pork sausages
- 2 x 400g/14oz tins cannellini beans
- 400g/14oz tinned chopped tomatoes
- 1 onion, chopped
- 2 red peppers, de-seeded & sliced
- 2 carrots, finely chopped
- 2 tbsp tomato puree/paste
- 1 tsp brown sugar
- 1 tsp dijon mustard
- 60ml/¼ cup vegetable stock
- Olive oil
- Salt & pepper to taste

THE METHOD

1 Preheat the oven to 200C/400F/Gas Mark 6

2 Brown the sausages, peppers, onions in a frying pan with a little oil for a few minutes, then slice the sausages into 1cm/½ inch slices.

3 Combine all the ingredients in an oven-proof dish and season.

4 Place in the oven and cook for 30-40 minutes or until the sausages are cooked through, the vegetables are tender and the stock is absorbed.

HYGGE HINT

Serve with slices of thick crusty bread & butter.

Bakes, Sweets & Jam

Recipes

Cookies For Company

SERVES FOUR

INGREDIENTS

- 350g/12oz flour
- 1 tsp bicarbonate of soda
- 1 tsp salt
- 225g/8oz butter
- 175g/6oz caster sugar
- 175g/6oz soft brown sugar
- 1 tsp vanilla extract
- 2 eggs
- 350g/12oz milk chocolate chips

HYGGE HINT

Allow plenty of space on the baking tray between the cookies as they will spread when baking and you don't want them to merge into each other. You may wish to make more than one batch of these. One or even two cookies is never enough when you have company!

THE METHOD

1 Preheat the oven to 190C/375F/Gas Mark 5.

2 Mix the flour, baking soda and salt together in a bowl.

3 Use a separate mixing bowl combine together the butter, sugar, brown sugar and vanilla extract until creamy. Add the eggs and gradually beat in the flour mixture. Stir in the chocolate chips and bring the dough together into a ball.

4 Roll the ball into a sausage 5cm in diameter. Cut the sausage into 2cm slices and lay on a baking tray

5 Bake in the preheated oven for 9-11 minutes.

6 Turn out onto to a wire rack to cool.

Ready-For-Tea Shortbread

SERVES FOUR

INGREDIENTS

- 200g/7oz unsalted butter, cubed
- 100g/3½oz sugar
- 1 tsp vanilla extract
- 300g/11oz plain flour

HYGGE HINT

Hot tea & fresh baked shortbread are a hygge classic combination. Have fun using different shaped cutters.

THE METHOD

1 Preheat the oven to 165C/325F/Gas Mark 3.

2 Line a baking tray with parchment.

3 Combine together the butter and sugar until smooth. Add the vanilla extract, then gently mix in the flour until completely incorporated.

4 Squeeze the mixture together to bring into a ball of dough.

5 Roll the dough out to a thickness of ½cm. Cut into shapes using a biscuit cutter.

6 Transfer the biscuits to the lined baking tray and chill 15 minutes.

7 Place in the oven and bake in the preheated oven for 15-20 minutes, or until golden-brown.

8 Turn out onto to a wire rack to cool.

Walnut Caramels

SERVES FOUR

INGREDIENTS

- 375g/13oz walnuts
- 125g/4oz butter
- 370ml/1½ cups double cream
- 1 tsp vanilla bean paste
- 400/14oz golden caster sugar
- 250ml/9oz golden syrup

HYGGE HINT

Sweet treats are hugely popular in Denmark and most associated with hygge. Take joy in the preparation of these crunchy walnut caramels - they're perfect with a lovely cup of hot coffee.

THE METHOD

1 Heat oven to 180C/350F fan/Gas Mark 4 and toast the walnuts on a baking sheet arranged in a single layer for 10 minutes. Meanwhile line a 15-20cm square tin with foil and grease with a little oil. Spread half the toasted nuts across the bottom of the tin.

2 In a saucepan, bring the butter, cream and vanilla to the boil, then remove from the heat.

3 In a separate saucepan, heat the sugar and syrup on a medium heat until it reaches 155C on a sugar thermometer. Do not stir or the sugar will ruin the texture.

4 Turn off the heat and gently add to the cream & vanilla mixture. Stir together and heat again until it reaches 125C on the thermometer. Remove from the heat and add the remaining nuts.

5 Tip everything into the tin. Leave to solidify for around 4 hours after-which it should be ready to cut into pieces. To cut the caramels use a hot knife – dip into boiling water between cuts.

Double Chocolate Pretzels

INGREDIENTS

- 400g/14oz milk chocolate, chopped
- 150g/5oz white chocolate, chopped
- 150g/5oz small salted pretzels

HYGGE HINT

Milk chocolate and white chocolate together - sinful? Yes! Scrumptious? Definitely! These are a real winner. Enjoy with a fun family board game.

THE METHOD

1 Use 2 glass bowls sitting over 2 saucepans of boiling water to gently melt the milk and white chocolate in separate bowls.

2 Line a 30cm x 20cm baking tray with baking parchment.

3 Pour the milk chocolate onto the paper then pour large dots of white chocolate on top.

4 Use a fork to swirl the white chocolate through the milk chocolate to create a marbled effect (don't overdo it though or you'll just mix it in).

5 Sit the pretzels on top and leave the chocolate to harden. When it's ready lift the parchment to tip the hardened chocolate sheet off the tray. Break into pieces to eat.

Coconut Truffle Bites

SERVES FOUR

INGREDIENTS

- 250ml/1 cup double cream
- 250g/9oz dark chocolate (at least 70% cocoa solids)
- 250g/9oz desiccated coconut

HYGGE HINT

Perfect for picnics or snacks in the park. These are the moments when memories are made.

THE METHOD

1 Break or chop the chocolate into small pieces

2 In a saucepan bring the cream to the boil and stir in the chocolate pieces until smooth.

3 Tip into a bowl. Cool for a few minutes, then place in the fridge for 1-2 hours or until the mixture has firmed up.

4 Scoop out teaspoons of the mixture and roll into small walnut-size balls with your hands.

5 Roll these chocolate balls onto a plate of desiccated coconut until completely covered. Eat straight away or store in an airtight box somewhere cool.

Marshmallow Mini Bites

SERVES FOUR

INGREDIENTS

- 1 bag of marshmallows
- 200g/7oz good quality milk chocolate broken up into pieces
- Mini cake cases

THE METHOD

1 Use a glass bowl sitting over a saucepan of boiling water to gently melt the milk chocolate.

2 Use a teaspoon to add a mound of melted chocolate to each cake case. Place the marshmallow on top and add another blob of chocolate to the top.

3 Leave to cool and get ready to eat as soon as the chocolate sets.

HYGGE HINT

So easy and just goes to prove that sometimes the simplest things can be superb. This is the perfect recipe to involve kids. They love marshmallows and chocolate and it's so easy for them to help. For more indulgence add a smartie to the top!

Chocolate Strawberry Fondue

INGREDIENTS

- 180ml/¾ cup single cream
- 200g/7oz milk chocolate, finely chopped
- 1 tbsp of unsalted butter
- Fresh strawberries (or your favourite fruit)
- Wooden skewers

THE METHOD

1 Remove and discard the green tops from the strawberries and put on a plate along with the wooden skewers.

2 Place the cream in a saucepan and gently heat until it starts simmering. Add the chocolate and whisk until it's melted and smooth. Add the butter and whisk this too until everything is silky.

3 Pour the melted chocolate fondue into a bowl. Set it out on the table with your plate of strawberries. Grab a strawberry on a stick, dip and dig in!

HYGGE HINT

Great as a dessert or serving after a summer barbecue. Keep the skewers for toasting marshmallows round the fire later in the evening.

Salted Caramel Choco Popcorn

SERVES FOUR

INGREDIENTS

- 3 tbsp vegetable oil
- 225g/8oz unpopped popcorn kernels
- 400g/14oz milk chocolate, chopped
- 4 tbsp salted caramel sauce

HYGGE HINT

Popcorn means movie night! Have a large bowl filled with the popcorn and pass it round.

THE METHOD

1 Gently heat the oil in a large saucepan for a minute or two.

2 Add the popcorn and shake the pot occasionally. When the popping sounds subside remove from the heat and pour the popcorn into a bowl.

3 Meanwhile use a glass bowl sitting over a saucepan of boiling water to gently melt the milk chocolate. Stir through the caramel sauce until it is combined with the chocolate.

4 Pour the caramel chocolate sauce into the bowl and combine to fully cover the popcorn.

5 Spread the chocolate popcorn in a single layer over the baking parchment and leave to harden.

Spiced Plum Jam

MAKES 4 JARS

INGREDIENTS

- 900g/2lb plumbs
- 120ml/½ cup water
- 1 tbsp lemon juice
- 900g/2lb jam sugar
- 1 tsp butter
- ¼ tsp ground nutmeg
- 1 tsp ground cinnamon

THE METHOD

1 Put the plums in a saucepan, add the water and gently simmer for 10-12 mins or until the plums are tender.

2 Add the lemon juice, sugar, butter, nutmeg & cinnamon and gently simmer for a few minutes until the sugar is dissolved.

3 Increase the heat and bring the jam to the boil for 20-25 minutes - until the setting point of 105C is reached. Do not stir.

4 Pour into sterilised jars. Leave to cool, label and seal.

HYGGE HINT

"The rule is jam tomorrow and jam yesterday, but never jam today"

Lewis Carroll

Easy Strawberry Jam

MAKES 4 JARS

INGREDIENTS

- 900g/2lb strawberries
- 3 tbsp lemon juice
- 900g/2lb jam sugar
- 1 tsp butter

HYGGE HINT

Sticky, sweet strawberry jam is the stuff of childhood memories. It's perfect with bread and butter, on a victoria sponge or with warm scones and clotted cream.

THE METHOD

1 Add the strawberries to a large saucepan along with the lemon juice. Bring to the boil and simmer for 5 minutes.

2 Tip in the sugar, stir over a very low heat until the sugar has completely dissolved. Then turn up the heat and bring back to the boil for 20-25 minutes - until the setting point of 105C is reached. Do not stir.

3 Remove from the heat stir in the butter and leave for 10 minutes to settle.

4 Pour into sterilised jars. Leave to cool, label and seal.

Spicy Tomato Chutney

MAKES 4 JARS

INGREDIENTS

- 250g/9oz red onions
- 500g/1lb 2oz tomatoes
- 1 fresh red chilli
- 60ml/¼ cup red wine vinegar
- 125g/5oz brown sugar

HYGGE HINT

Hygge gatherings always find a need for chutney whether it is with a selection of cheese and cured meat, as a relish for a burger at a barbecue or mixed with Greek yoghurt as dip.

THE METHOD

1 Peel and chop the onions.

2 Chop the tomatoes. De-seed and finely slice the chilli.

3 Add everything to the pan, combine and simmer 40 minutes until you get a chutney type consistency.

4 Check the balance of the vinegar & sugar and add a little more of either if needed.

5 Pour into sterilised jars. Leave to cool, label and seal.

Chilli Jam

MAKES 4 JARS

INGREDIENTS

- 8 red peppers
- 10 red chillies
- 750g/1lb 11oz jam sugar
- 250ml/1 cup cider vinegar

THE METHOD

1 De-seed the peppers & chillies and finely chop.

2 Take a saucepan and dissolve the sugar in the vinegar over a low heat without stirring.

3 Add the chopped peppers and chillies to the pan. Bring to the boil and keep it boiling for 10 minutes. Again don't stir.

4 Take the pan off the heat and allow to cool for half an hour.

5 Pour into sterilised jars. Leave to cool, label and seal.

HYGGE HINT

Lovely served as a canapé with warmed savoury biscuits and a glass of red wine. You could also use pretty jars and hand written labels to give away as gifts.

Simple Rosemary Bread

SERVES FOUR

INGREDIENTS

- 500g/1lb 2oz strong white flour
- 2 tsp salt
- 7g sachet fast-action yeast
- 3 tbsp olive oil
- 310ml/1¼ cups water
- 2 tsp freshly chopped rosemary

HYGGE HINT

Making bread is so therapeutic. The kneading of the dough is rhythmic and calming and not to be rushed. It's mindfulness in the kitchen and should be savoured. This lovely bread goes perfectly with Dutch Gouda cheese. Try taking out the rosemary and using this bread as a companion to hygge homemade jam.

THE METHOD

1 Mix the flour, salt and yeast in a large bowl. Make a hollow in the centre and add the oil and water. Add the rosemary and combine well to form a dough.

2 Lightly flour the worktop and knead the dough for 5 minutes or until it no longer feels sticky (add a little more flour if needed). Place the 'worked' dough in a lightly oiled bowl. Leave to 'prove' for 1 hour, during which time it should double in size. Meanwhile line a baking tray with baking parchment.

3 Add a little more flour to the work surface. Take the dough out of the bowl and fold it repeatedly in on itself using the heels of your hands until it is smooth and the air is knocked out. Mould into a ball and place on the baking tray to 'prove' for an hour until doubled in size again. Heat oven to 200C/400F/Gas Mark 6.

4 Dust the loaf with flour and make a cross about 6cm long into the top of the loaf with a sharp knife. Bake for 25-30 mins until golden brown. Leave to cool on a wire rack.

Cheese Scones

SERVES FOUR

INGREDIENTS

- 200g/7oz self raising flour
- pinch of salt
- pinch of cayenne pepper
- 50g/2oz butter
- 75g/3oz mature cheddar cheese, grated
- 120ml/½ cup milk

HYGGE HINT

Best served warm with company

THE METHOD

1 Heat the oven to 220C/425F/Gas 7.

2 Place some baking parchment on a baking tray.

3 Combine together the flour and salt and use your thumbs & fingers to rub in the butter.

4 Add the cheese, stir in the milk and bring together into a dough.

5 Place the dough on a floured work surface and pat it down until it's about an inch thick.

6 Use a cutter to make 2inch rounds, brush with milk and bake for 10-15 until well risen and golden. When they are done, remove from the oven and tip out on a wire rack to cool.

Drinks

Recipes

Luxury Hot Chocolate

SERVES TWO

INGREDIENTS

- 500ml/2 cups milk
- 120ml/½ cup double cream
- 75g/3oz chocolate curls

THE METHOD

1 Combine the milk, double cream and chocolate curls into a pan and gently bring to the boil.

2 Throughout the heating process whisk until smooth.

3 Serve in two mugs topped with mini marshmallows and a few extra chocolate curls.

HYGGE HINT

You can't get much more hygge than this. There are so many perfect situations that call for hot chocolate - coming in from the cold, with cake, before bed. Add a straw for extra fun!

Salted Caramel Hot Chocolate

SERVES TWO

INGREDIENTS

- 500ml/2 cups milk
- 120ml/½ cup single cream
- 4 tbsp salted caramel sauce
- 125g/4oz dark chocolate, finely chopped

THE METHOD

1 Combine the milk, cream, caramel sauce and chocolate pieces into a pan and gently bring to the boil. Whisk until smooth.

2 Serve in two mugs topped extra salted caramel sauce and/or fresh squirty cream.

HYGGE HINT

A more grown up hot chocolate - ideal for contemplating life by the fire with a blanket.

Mulled Wine For Sharing

SERVES FOUR

INGREDIENTS

- 1 bottle good red wine (treat yourself)
- 1 fresh orange, quartered
- 75g/3oz brown sugar
- 2 whole cloves
- 1 cinnamon stick
- 1 star anise
- ¼ tsp nutmeg
- 2 dried bay leaf

THE METHOD

1 Put the wine in a saucepan along with the quartered orange, sugar, cloves, cinnamon stick, star anise, nutmeg and bay leaves.

2 Gently heat through until all the sugar has dissolved and the wine fills the kitchen with its delicious warming aroma.

3 Remove from the heat. Strain the wine through a sieve and serve in steaming mugs.

HYGGE HINT

A real festive treat, mulled wine always helps create a cheerful mood. Lovely inside for an informal gathering of friends or outdoors marvelling at the light of the moon.

Spiced Vanilla Cider

SERVES FOUR

INGREDIENTS

- 1lt/4 cups dry cider
- 1 vanilla pod, halved
- 4 tbsp fresh orange juice
- 75g/3oz brown sugar
- Seeds of 1 pomegranate
- 1 cardamom pods,
- 2 star anise

THE METHOD

1 Put all the ingredients in a saucepan and bring to the boil.

2 Reduce the heat and gently simmer for 5 minutes.

3 Make sure the balance of spices and sweetness is right - add a little more sugar if needed.

4 Remove from the heat. Strain the cider through a sieve and serve in steaming mugs or heatproof glasses.

HYGGE HINT

A twist on mulled wine, the sweetness of the cider and pomegranate marry effortlessly in this winter warming tipple.

Cakes & Puddings

Recipes

Classic Cappuccino Cake

SERVES SIX

INGREDIENTS

- 250g/9oz softened butter
- 250g/9oz caster sugar
- 300g/11oz self-raising flour
- 4 eggs
- 200ml very strong coffee, cooled
- 500g/1lb 2oz tub mascarpone
- 2 tsp brown sugar
- 75g/3oz icing sugar
- 1 tbsp cocoa powder

HYGGE HINT

If there are two things near the top of the hygge list it would coffee and cake. Combine them together and you have the ultimate hygge treat.

THE METHOD

1 Heat oven to 180C/350F/Gas Mark 4. Grease and line two 20cm cake tins.

2 Beat the butter and caster sugar until smooth and creamy. Add the flour and eggs, Carry on beating until everything is smooth and well combined.

3 Add 100ml of the coffee and fold through the mixture. Divide into 2 cake tins and bake for 25-30 mins or until risen and golden.

4 When they are cool enough to touch take the sponges out of the tins and leave to cool on a wire rack. Whilst the cakes are cooling, make the icing.

5 Add the brown sugar to the rest of the coffee. Tip the mascarpone into a large bowl and beat in the icing sugar and remaining coffee until smooth and creamy.

6 Use about half of this inside the cake to bring the sponges together. Use the rest as a topping with the cocoa powder sieved over the top to gently dust the cake.

Three Tier Red Velvet Cake

SERVES SIX

INGREDIENTS

Sponge Ingredients:
- 250g/9oz softened unsalted butter
- 200g/7oz dark chocolate, chopped
- 500g/1lb2oz plain flour
- 500g/1lb2oz golden caster sugar
- 2 tbsp cocoa powder
- 1 tsp bicarbonate of soda
- ½ tsp salt
- 2 large eggs
- 200g/7oz Greek yogurt
- 400g/14oz cooked beetroot (not pickled beetroot)
- 4 tbsp red food colouring
- 120ml/ ½ cup boiling water

Icing Ingredients:
- 200g/7oz soft cheese
- 250g/9oz softened unsalted butter
- 400g/14oz icing sugar
- 2 tsp vanilla extract

HYGGE HINT

Savour every moment as you create this regal tower of cake. Enlist the help of a friend or family member to make it fun.

THE METHOD

1 Heat oven to 180C/350F/Gas Mark 4. Grease and line three 20cm cake tins. Gently melt the butter and chocolate together in a saucepan.

2 Meanwhile mix the flour, sugar, cocoa, soda and salt in a large mixing bowl.

3 In a food processor whizz up the egg, yogurt and beetroot until smooth. Tip the beetroot mix into the flour bowl along with the melted chocolate, boiling water & food colouring, mix well.

4 Divide evenly into the 3 cake tins and bake for 25-30 mins or until risen and firm to the touch. When they are cool enough to touch take the sponges out of the tins and leave to cool on a wire rack. Whilst the cakes are cooling, make the icing.

5 Tip the soft cheese and butter into a large bowl. Mix well and then combine in the icing sugar and vanilla extract. Use about half of this inside the cake layers to bring the sponges together. Use the rest as a topping.

Carrot & Walnut Cake

SERVES SIX

INGREDIENTS

- 430ml/1¾ cups vegetable oil
- 400g/14oz plain flour
- 2 tsp bicarbonate of soda
- 550g/1¼lb sugar
- 5 eggs
- ½ tsp salt
- 2½ tsp ground cinnamon
- 500g/1lb 2oz carrots, grated
- 200g/7oz cream cheese
- 150g/5oz caster sugar
- 100g/3½oz butter, softened
- Finely grated zest of 1 orange
- 10 walnuts, halved

HYGGE HINT

Carrot cake is truly delicious comfort food.

THE METHOD

1 Heat oven to 165C/325F/Gas Mark 3. Grease and line a 30cm cake tin.

2 Beat the oil, flour, soda, sugar, eggs, salt & cinnamon together until smooth and creamy. Add the carrots and fold through until well combined.

3 Tip into the cake tin and bake for 60-70 mins or until risen and firm to the touch.

4 When it is cool enough to touch take the sponge out of the tin and leave to cool on a wire rack. Whilst the cakes are cooling, make the icing.

5 Tip the cream cheese, caster sugar, butter and orange zest into a large bowl and beat until smooth and creamy.

6 Spread this over the top of the completely cooled sponge and decorate with the walnuts halves.

Luxury Rice Pudding

SERVES FOUR

INGREDIENTS

- 50g/2oz butter
- 125g/4oz pudding rice
- 75g/3oz caster sugar
- 1.12 litre/4½ cups milk
- 120ml/½ cup cream
- 1 tsp vanilla extract
- ¼ tsp grated nutmeg
- 75g/3oz blueberries
- 1 banana, sliced

HYGGE HINT

There's something delightfully old fashioned about rice pudding. It's been loved through generations and for good reason. Place the pudding straight from the oven onto the centre of the kitchen table with a large spoon for everyone to help themselves.

THE METHOD

1 Preheat the oven to 140C/275F/Gas Mark 1.

2 Melt the butter in a saucepan on a medium heat. Add the rice and combine well. Add the sugar and stir through until dissolved.

3 Pour in the milk and continue stirring for a couple of minutes before adding the cream and vanilla essence.

4 Once the pan is gently simmering and all the lumps have disappeared put this into an oven proof dish,

5 Sprinkle with nutmeg and bake for 1-1½ hours.

6 When it's ready serve with sliced bananas and fresh blueberries.

Fruit Crumble

SERVES FOUR

INGREDIENTS

Crumble Ingredients:
- 200g/7oz plain flour
- 75g/3oz caster sugar
- 100g/3½oz butter at room temperature, cut into pieces

Filling Ingredients:
- 120ml/½ cup water
- 50g/2oz caster sugar
- 400g/14oz apples, peeled, cored & cubed
- 50g/2oz unsalted butter
- 125g/4oz blackberries
- ¼ tsp ground cinnamon

HYGGE HINT

Fruit crumble is so comforting and versatile too, both as a summer or winter pudding making use of the best fruits in season. Try serving with a dash of milk, cream, vanilla ice cream or custard.

THE METHOD

1 Preheat the oven to 200°C/400°F/ Gas Mark 6.

2 Sift the flour into a bowl and add the sugar. Use your thumbs and forefingers to rub the butter through the flour mixture to make the crumble topping. The texture should be like breadcrumbs.

3 To make the filling, boil the water and sugar together in a saucepan. Add the fruit. Simmer for 3 minutes.

4 Spread the fruit into an oven-proof dish and sprinkle the crumble over the top.

5 Bake in the preheated oven for 25 to 30 minutes until the apples are tender and the crumble is golden.

Bread & Butter Pudding

SERVES FOUR

INGREDIENTS

- 50g butter
- 5 slices bread
- 3 eggs
- 180ml/¾ cup double cream
- 250ml/1 cup milk
- 1 tsp vanilla extract
- Large pinch of nutmeg and ground cinnamon
- 3 tbsp brown sugar

THE METHOD

1 Preheat the oven to 165C/325F/Gas Mark 3 and grease a baking dish with a little butter.

2 Butter the bread and cut the slices in half diagonally. Arrange them in the dish, buttered side up.

3 In a bowl, whisk together the eggs, cream, milk, vanilla, nutmeg and cinnamon. Pour over the top of the bread and sprinkle with caster sugar.

4 Bake in the oven for 25-35 minutes or until the pudding is set and gently browned on top.

HYGGE HINT

The great thing about this recipe is you'll nearly always have all the ingredients and it's the perfect way to use up the last of the bread (bread a few days old is even better).

Giant Pavlova

SERVES SIX

INGREDIENTS

Meringue Ingredients:
- 8 eggs
- 500g/1lb 2oz caster sugar
- 2 tsp white wine vinegar
- 2 tsp cornflour
- 1½ tsp vanilla extract

Topping Ingredients:
- 600g/1lb 5oz strawberries
- 5 tbsp icing sugar
- 750ml/3 cups double cream

HYGGE HINT

You will always hear exclamations of 'Wow' and 'amazing' when a pavlova comes out. Everyone loves it. It's great for a dinner dessert or piled into bowls in front of the tv.

THE METHOD

1 Heat oven to 140C/275F/Gas Mark 1.

2 Separate the yolks from the whites and put the whites in a squeaky clean bowl. Whisk until they form stiff peaks (an electric hand mixer is best), then whisk in the sugar a little at a time followed by the vinegar, cornflour and vanilla.

3 Spread the meringue in a circle shape on a piece of baking parchment (the circle should be about the size of a dinner plate)

4 Bake for 1hr, turn off the oven and leave the pavlova to cool inside the oven.

5 Meanwhile make the topping by slicing the strawberries and combining with the icing sugar.

6 Whip the cream until it's stiff then spread this over the completely cooled meringue. Arrange the sliced strawberries over the top and serve.

Spiced Banana Bread

SERVES SIX

INGREDIENTS

- 140g/4½oz golden caster sugar
- 140g/4½oz butter
- 140g/4½oz self-raising flour
- 2 eggs
- ½ tsp mixed spice
- 1 tsp baking powder
- 2 ripe bananas

HYGGE HINT

Slice and arrange on a plate then invite a friend round for a cuppa. If you have a teapot, put the kettle on and make a pot. If you have a tea-cosy - perfect!

THE METHOD

1 Heat oven to 180C/350F/Gas Mark 4.

2 Butter a 2lb loaf tin and line the base and sides with baking parchment.

3 Peel the bananas and use the back of a fork to mash them well.

4 Crack the eggs into a cup and beat for a few seconds.

5 Cream the butter and sugar together and fold in the eggs, flour, mixed spice & baking powder.

6 Gently combine the bananas into the mixture. Pour into the prepared tin and bake for about 25-30 minutes or until a wooden skewer comes out clean when prodded into the bread.

7 Allow the tin to cool for a few minutes then turn the loaf out onto a wire rack. Slice and serve whilst still warm with lashings of real butter spread on each slice.

Sticky Ginger Cake

SERVES EIGHT

INGREDIENTS

- 50g/2oz unsalted butter
- 125g/4oz light brown sugar
- 400g/14oz golden syrup
- 1 teaspoon ground ginger
- 1 teaspoon ground cinnamon
- 250ml/1 cup full-fat milk
- 2 eggs, beaten
- 1 tsp bicarbonate of soda
- 2 tbsp warm water
- 300g/11oz plain flour

HYGGE HINT

Although the hygge factor applies to ginger anytime of year it's particularly felt around Christmas time.

THE METHOD

1 Preheat the oven to 165C/325F/ Gas Mark 3 and line a 30cm x 20cm baking tin with baking parchment.

2 Gently melt together the butter sugar, syrup & ginger in a saucepan. Whilst this is warming through dissolve the soda in the warm water.

3 In a separate bowl combine together the milk and eggs.

4 Take the saucepan off the heat and combine the egg mixture and dissolved bicarbonate of soda into the pan.

5 Add the flour to a large mixing bowl and pour in the contents of the saucepan. Mix well then tip this smooth liquid batter into the lined tin.

6 Place in the preheated oven and cook for 50 minutes or until firm to the touch on top.

7 Leave to cool and then slice into squares. Delicious.

Pear Pudding

SERVES SIX

INGREDIENTS

- 200g/7oz melted butter
- 200g/7oz caster sugar
- 4 eggs, beaten
- 75g/3oz plain flour
- 3 tbsp cocoa powder
- 400g/14oz tinned pears

HYGGE HINT

Serve with lots of cream or custard.

THE METHOD

1 Preheat the oven to 190C/170C fan/ gas 5.

2 Grease a Lightly shallow ovenproof dish. Combine together the melted butter and sugar then whisk in the eggs.

3 Use a sieve to add the flour and cocoa powder to the egg mixture and mix beat really well.

4 Drain the pears and arrange in the ovenproof dish. Pour the pudding mixture over the top and bake in the centre of the oven for 40-50 mins or until the mixture is firm on top and gooey inside.

Hygge Craft

Creating a hygge atmosphere at home is a joy and much easier to achieve than you may think. Sometimes simply re-arranging some key home furnishings will create a beautiful cosy hygge nook in your home which will all at once feel warm, cosy and safe.

These simple suggestions can help you make the most of your surroundings from key lighting and fabrics to crafting simple homemade gifts and accessories that you can make with family or friends.

Autumn Leaf Light

YOU'LL NEED

- 1 empty jar
- A handful of fallen Autumn leaves
- Glue dots
- PVA glue
- Paint brush
- Tea-light

HYGGE HINT

This is a really easy idea to make your home feel Autumn cosy. Use fresh leaves so that they are bendy and easy to work with - old leaves will be crispy and break up easily. As this is a naked flame never leave it unattended.

INSTRUCTIONS

1 Arrange your leaves on the outside of the jam jar using the glue dots. You don't need to completely cover the jar with leaves, it's nice to be able to see the outline of individual leaves rather than just a mass (small leaves are best for this).

2 Once you have got your leaves in the right position completely cover them, and every inch of the outside of the jar, with glue using the brush. This will really secure the leaves to the jar and give you a lovely blurry/glassy effect once the glue dries off.

3 Drop the tea light into the bottom of the jam jar then when night falls and it's time to get cosy, light up the tea-light and enjoy the Autumn glow.

Custom Made Jar Candle

HYGGE CRAFT

YOU'LL NEED

- 200g/7oz candle wax flakes
- 1 tablespoon ground cinnamon
- 1 tablespoon vanilla extract
- 1 candle wick
- 1 jam-size glass jar

HYGGE HINT

Vanilla and cinnamon work really well together but you can alter the scents to whatever you wish.
If you like you can also wrap a ribbon around the jar to make it look especially pretty.

INSTRUCTIONS

1 Gently heat a glass bowl over a pan of simmering water on the cooker and add the wax flakes. When it starts melting add the cinnamon and vanilla. Carry on very gently heating until everything is melted and combined.

2 Meanwhile prepare your candle wick. Place the metal end of the wick so it rests inside the bottom of the jar. Wrap the top of the wick around a wood skewer or pencil and balance the skewer across the mouth of the jar to hold the wick in place while your candle sets. (Make sure the metal part is still resting on the base of the jar).

3 When the wax is melted and you have an even colour pour it into the jar being careful not to disturb the wick.

4 Leave to set overnight and then when it's ready unwind the wick from the pencil and trim it with some scissors so you have just a little of the wick showing at the top of the candle.

Fairylight Mason Jar

HYGGE CRAFT

YOU'LL NEED

- 1 mason jar with lid
- PVA glue
- Strong Sticky tape
- Paint brush
- Battery powered fairylights

HYGGE HINT

This really is so easy to do. It's quick and simple but has a magical feel. Dot them around your hygge home.

INSTRUCTIONS

1 Using the brush paint the inside of the jar with glue, make sure you cover every inch then let it dry off.

2 Stick the battery part of the led lights to the inside of the lid using the sticky tape.

3 Arrange the lights inside the jar, turn them on and close over the lid. Sit and enjoy the lovely warm glassy light.

Decorated Drift Wood Display

HYGGE CRAFT

YOU'LL NEED

- Driftwood sticks
- Brightly coloured paint
- Paintbrush
- Glass vase
- A long shoreline walk

HYGGE HINT

This is a great way to turn any driftwood finds into a natural hygge home display. Make the colours really bold and you'll love the vibe they add to the room.

INSTRUCTIONS

1 Lay the sticks out and take some time painting bright colours on each of them.

2 Because the sea and sun have bleached the wood you'll find it has a smooth yet uneven surface that is really nice to work with. Try painting rings around each stick in colourful bold stripes.

3 When they have dried, load them into a glass vase to make a really beautiful and bright natural room decoration.

Cozy Stargazing

YOU'LL NEED

- A clear night
- Some good friends & family
- A ground sheet/blanket
- Some really comfy warm blankets & pillows

HYGGE HINT

Fire up the chiminea, grab some spiced cider and make a night of it.

INSTRUCTIONS

1 When the sun goes down get yourself out into the garden. Lay out the ground sheet and get set up with your blankets and pillows.

2 Lie flat on your back and look out into space. If you're lucky you'll see a shooting star.

3 Take time to look carefully at the stars and you'll start seeing the patterns they make. Look for some of the well known constellations like The Bear, The Big Dipper, The 7 Sisters and of course The North Star which is one of the brightest stars in the sky.

4 Lie back and take it all in.

Pocket Hand Warmers

HYGGE CRAFT

YOU'LL NEED

- 2 x 4 inch squares of your favourite fabric
- Fabric scissors
- Needle & thread
- Pins
- Uncooked rice or barley

HYGGE HINT

These pretty hand warmers will keep hands cosy on a winters day. They are a welcome companion for a lovely walk on a cold day.

THE METHOD

1 Place the two squares of fabric on top of each other with the patterns facing (this will be turned inside out after sewing to reveal the pattern). Use pins to keep in place and a sew a seam approx. ¼ inch from the edge.

2 Turn the pouch inside out and pop out the corners.

3 Carefully fill the pouch ¾ full through the gap with the rice or barley.

4 Use a pin to temporarily close the gap while you sew the pouch shut.

5 Trim off any untidy edges.

6 To warm up, heat in the microwave for approx. 20 seconds but be sure to check the temperature before allowing children to handle.

Pine Cone Fire-lighters

HYGGE CRAFT

YOU'LL NEED

- The ends of all your burned down candles. You can mix colours together or if you prefer you can use a new candle or buy candle wax.
- Long Candle wicks
- Dry pine cones
- Greaseproof paper

HYGGE HINT

These are fun to collect on a long walk in a forest and can double as a lovely table decoration. Try experimenting with different colours and add candle fragrance.

INSTRUCTIONS

1 Begin my melting your old candles in a bowl over a pan of boiling water until all the wax has liquidised then remove from the heat.

2 Cut a length of wick long enough to fully wrap around your pine cone leaving a wick sticking out from the side. Do this for all the pine cones.

3 Lay out a sheet of greaseproof paper. The candle wax should start to thicken as it cools. Use a large spoon to dip the cones into the wax ensuring they are completely covered including the wick and place on the greaseproof paper to cool and dry.

Log Tea Light Holders

HYGGE CRAFT

YOU'LL NEED

- Hand saw
- Power drill
- 1½ inch wood drill bit
- Tea light candles
- Logs of differing lengths at least 5 inches in diameter and no more than 12 inches in height

INSTRUCTIONS

1 Use the saw to make sure the logs have even ends so that they can safely stand up on either end.

2 Drill a single hole to a depth of approximately 1/2" in the surface of one end of the stump.

3 Put the tea light in the hole and make sure the log is really stable.

4 If you do a few of these and bunch them together (different heights of logs works best) you have lovely display which will work inside you house or out.

5 Always be careful having naked flames in your home and always remember to extinguish them properly.

HYGGE HINT

Logs are soooooo hygge. Use birch logs if you can as these have a lovely bleached bark effect.

Hygge Yoga

Hygge yoga is the pursuit of comfort within ourselves.

Can Yoga Be Hygge?

Yoga takes you into the present moment, the only place where life exists.

Yoga is an ancient form of practice that focuses on strength, flexibility and breathing. Originating in India more than 5,000 years ago, yoga helps boost physical & mental wellbeing and has been adopted by cultures around the world.

Yoga is meant to make you feel good. It's not a competitive sport. This routine is designed to relax you and take you on a personal journey. Always listen to your body and never push yourself too hard - that would completely go against the spirit of hygge. Move into poses on a breath exhalation and make sure you move slowly and methodically.

To really enjoy this session you must set the scene. Arrange some quiet time for yourself. Make sure the room is really warm and comfortable. Dim the lighting & light some candles. Yoga will help you be in the moment. Being present in the moment is part of what hygge is all about.

When you are practicing yoga try to empty your mind of any thoughts. That is not as easy as it sounds, but have patience with yourself. If you try to anchor your thoughts around your breathing you will learn to calm your mind and move towards a stillness which will benefit your well-being and bring a new meaning to hygge.

Enjoy your journey.

Relaxation Routine

This gentle routine is ideal for preparing for bed, winding down in the evening or if you wish to meditate/rest throughout the day. You will need to have a mat and some pillows to hand and it should take no more than 30 minutes.

Pose 1: *Cow*

Pose 2: *Cat*

Pose 3: *Bridge Pose*

Pose 4: *Legs Up The Wall*

Pose 5: *Seated Forward Bend*

Pose 6: *Wide Leg Forward Bend*

Pose 7: *Cobra*

Pose 8: *Left Nostril Breathing*

Cow

Come onto your hands and knees with hips placed over the knees. Shoulders positioned over the wrists. Your knees and hands should be shoulder distance apart, and the spine neutral. On exhalation gently lift your tail bone up to the sky, let your belly drop toward the mat and look up. Hold for a few moments before going into the next pose.

Cat

On a breath exhalation, lengthen your tail bone to the ground, draw the belly up to the spine and round the upper back like a cat. Concentrate on pressing your hands into the mat to open the shoulder blades. Let the head drop. Gently and slowly move through ten rounds of Cat/Cow, then return to a neutral spine.

Bridge Pose

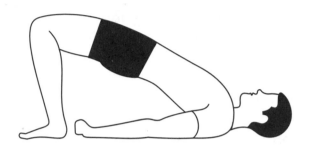

On your mat lie down with feet flat on the floor hip-width apart. Place your hands beside you with palms facing down. Engage your thighs and core and on exhalation lift your body up so that your back is flat and your knees are at a 45 degree angle whilst your arms remain flat on the floor. Settle into the pose and hold it for 2-3 minutes if you can.

Legs Up The Wall

Position yourself on your mat side-on close up to wall. Roll onto your back with your legs up in the air. Twist yourself around 90 degrees so that your legs rest straight up against the wall. Shuffle your bottom up tight against the wall if you need to. Keep your arms straight by your side with the palms flat down. Remain in this pose for 5 minutes breathing deeply and slowly, concentrating on nothing other than movement and feeling of your breath.

Seated Forward Bend

Sit on the mat with your legs straight out in front of you. Place pillow(s) on your thighs against your stomach (you may need to experiment with the height of the support). Put your arms above your head then reach forward as you bend your body onto the pillow and rest the side of your head onto the pillow support. Allow your arms to rest by your side and remain in this position for 5 minutes.

Wide Leg Forward Bend

This is a variation on the last pose. This time move your legs apart whilst you are in an upright sitting position. Place your cushion(s) onto the floor between your legs. Put your arms above your head then reach forward as you bend your body onto the pillow and rest the side of your head onto the pillow support – use the opposite side of your head from the last pose. Allow your arms to rest by your side and remain in this position for 5 minutes. If this feels uncomfortable it can be helpful to sit on a block or cushion to lift your pelvis or/and you may wish to bend your knees a little.

Cobra

Lie face-down on mat. With elbows bent place palms a little away from each side of your body in line with the breastbone. Come onto fingertips and point elbows toward sky and out to sides Press pelvis, toes, and fingertips into floor. On exhalation straighten the arms enough to lift the chest off the mat. Keep the spine long and tip the head back. Hold for 8 full deep breaths before relaxing back onto the mat.

Left Nostril Breathing

Sit in a comfortable cross- legged position. Keep your back straight with your shoulders low down away from your ears. Try to imagine a piece of string being pulled from above lifting the crown of your head up towards the sky. Cover your right nostril with your thumb or finger and begin breathing in and out through your left nostril. Breathe like this for at least 2 minutes.

This may seem strange but breathing through the left nostril has a calming effect on the nervous system and aids mediation and restful sleep.

other

COOKNATION TITLES

CookNation is the leading publisher of innovative and practical recipe books for the modern cook.

To find out more and to browse the full catalogue please visit:

www.cooknationbooks.com
www.bellmackenzie.com

 CookNation